Blue-Ringed Octopuses

BY ELIZABETH RAUM

AMICUS HIGH INTEREST 🦴 AMICUS INK

Amicus High Interest and Amicus Ink are imprints of Amicus
P.O. Box 1329, Mankato, MN 56002
www.amicuspublishing.us

Library of Congress Cataloging-in-Publication Data
Raum, Elizabeth, author.
 Blue-ringed octopuses / by Elizabeth Raum.
 pages cm. — (Poisonous animals)
 Audience: K to grade 3.
 Includes bibliographical references and index. 1 - 32
 ISBN 978-1-60753-785-4 (library binding)
 ISBN 1-60753-785-0 (library binding)
 ISBN 978-1-60753-884-4 (ebook)
 ISBN 978-1-68152-036-0 (paperback)
Summary: This photo-illustrated book for elementary readers
describes the venomous blue-ringed octopus of the Pacific
and Indian oceans. Readers learn how these octopi use their
colorful rings or stripes to warn predators and how they use
venom to kill their prey. Also explains where they live and what
to do when they are encountered.
1. Blue-ringed octopuses—Juvenile literature. 2. Poisonous
marine invertebrates—Juvenile literature. 3. Children's questions
and answers. I. Title.
 QL430.3.O2R38 2016
 594.56—dc23
                                        2014033277

Editor: Wendy Dieker
Series Designer: Kathleen Petelinsek
Book Designer: Heather Dreisbach
Photo Researcher: Kurtis Kinneman

Photo Credits: Alamy/Marcus Quartly cover; Alamy/
imageBROKER 10-11; Alamy/Barry Turner 12; Corbis/Bernard
Radvaner 15; Corbis/Fred Bavendam/Minden Pictures 24;
Getty Images/Richard Merritt FRPS 8; National Geographic
Creative/David Doubilet 23; SeaPics 7; Shutterstock/
orlandin 5; Shutterstock/Jette Vis 16-17; Shutterstock/Richard
Whitcombe 19, 28; Shutterstock/totograph 20; Shutterstock/
Sergiy Zavgorodny 27

HC 10 9 8 7 6 5 4 3 2
PB 10 9 8 7 6 5 4 3 2 1

Table of Contents

WITHDRAWN

Beautiful but Deadly

A small octopus crawls through a **tide pool**. It is tan. Dark brown circles mark its skin. A rock hits the water. In a flash, bright blue circles appear. They seem to glow. Don't pick it up! It's a blue-ringed octopus. Its bite is full of **venom**, a kind of poison. It can kill.

A blue-ringed octopus shows its blue rings when it is scared.

These octopuses are tiny. Most are about the size of a golf ball. Their bodies are less than 2 inches (5 cm) long. Their arms reach about 3 inches (7.5 cm). Few people see them. They might startle the octopus and see a flash of blue. How pretty! They reach for it. Oh, no! That's when the blue-ring bites.

 How big are baby blue-rings?

This tiny baby blue-ring will grow to the size of a golf ball.

 They are about the size of a grape seed.

The blue-ringed octopus is small.
It can fit in your hand.

 Do blue-rings hunt people?

8

Blue-ring venom is called **TTX**. It works quickly. It attacks the muscles. People who are bitten become **paralyzed**. They cannot move. They cannot talk. They cannot breathe. If doctors help them breathe, they will live. In a day or two, they will be fine.

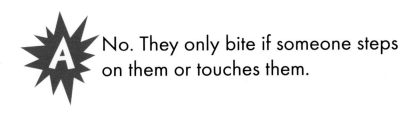
No. They only bite if someone steps on them or touches them.

Finding Food

Blue-rings are tan, yellow, or pink. They have darker rings or stripes. Blue-rings wait for **prey** to come to them. Their colors help them hide from prey. A crab walks past. It never sees the blue-ring. The blue-ring reaches out and grabs the crab. Rows of suckers on the blue-ring's arm are like suction cups. They hold the prey.

This small crab will make a good meal for a blue-ring.

Take a close look under the blue-ring's body. The mouth is in the middle of the suckers.

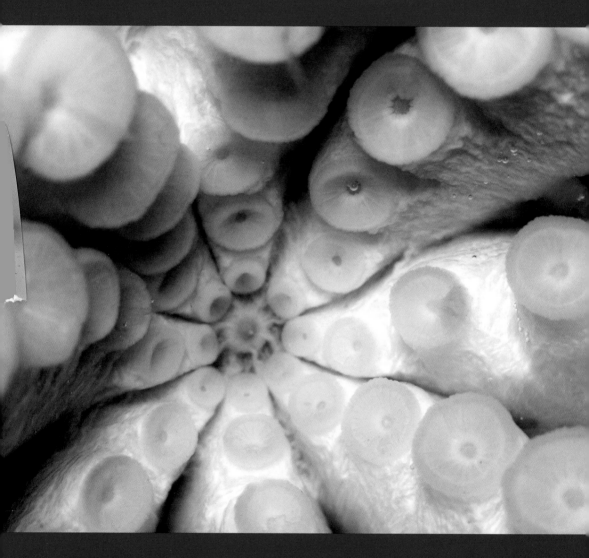

 Q What do blue-ringed octopuses eat?

The blue-ring's mouth is on the bottom of its body. It has a sharp, parrot-like beak. It punches a hole in the prey's shell. Then it spits its venom into the hole. The venom works fast. It kills the prey. It turns the prey's insides to mush. The blue-ring sucks out the juices. Yum!

 Small crabs, hermit crabs, shrimp, and small fish.

Staying Alive

Blue-ringed octopuses are very shy. They would rather hide than fight. They don't have any bones, so they can squeeze into small spaces. Blue-rings hide between rocks. They hide in underground holes. They burrow into the sand. Sometimes they hide in old bottles or cans. **Predators** can't see them. Neither can people.

Octopuses often live alone. They try to keep other animals away.

16

These octopuses have another
trick. They can change
color quickly to match their
surroundings. Special **organs**
in their body help them do this.
Blue-rings take on the color of
rocks, plants, or sand. But when
they are bothered, bright blue
rings or stripes appear.
It's a warning. Stay away!

A blue-ring's color matches the
ocean floor until it is bothered.

Bright blue rings or stripes mean danger. The warning works. Most animals have learned to stay away. People are learning, too. No other octopus has venom as strong as TTX. Even so, blue-rings are not safe from predators. Moray eels and peacock mantis shrimp eat them. So do sharks and other large fish.

 Does the venom make predators like eels sick?

Moray eels are one of only a few animals that eat blue-rings.

 No. Over time, their bodies have changed so that TTX does not affect them.

Blue-rings live in tide pools along the coasts of Australia and Japan.

At Home in the Ocean

Most blue-ringed octopuses live near land in the Pacific and Indian Oceans. They live up to 164 feet (50 meters) below the ocean's surface. Often, they live in tide pools. Tide pools are rocky pools beside the ocean. When the tide is high, the pools fill with water. When the tide is low, they look like small puddles.

Blue-rings crawl on the ocean bottom. They can also swim. Special jet power helps them swim fast. Seawater enters their bodies. It washes past their two **gills**. Strong muscles squirt it out through a funnel or tube. This strong jet of water speeds them along. They swim away from danger.

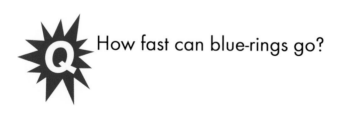 How fast can blue-rings go?

Blue-rings use jet power to move quickly through the water.

 They go about 1 foot (30.5 cm) a second.

Female blue-rings carry their eggs until they hatch.

 Why does the mother die after the eggs hatch?

Blue-rings live a year or less. Each female lays 50 to 100 eggs before she dies. She holds them in her arms until they hatch. It takes about a month. The babies grow quickly. They swim in the ocean for another month. Then they are adults. They settle to the ocean floor to hunt.

 She does not eat while holding the eggs.

Blue-Rings
and Humans

There is still much to learn about blue-ringed octopuses. **Biologists** are scientists who study living things. They want to learn more about blue-rings. They study blue-rings in labs. They study them in the ocean. They want to know more about the blue-ring's life cycle. They want to know more about TTX. What is it made of? Does it have other uses?

Scuba divers look for
blue-rings in the ocean.

Blue-ringed octopuses have a good home in the ocean.

Some people want to keep blue-rings as pets. A few pet stores sell them. But owning a blue-ring is a bad idea. Pet owners risk a deadly bite. Read about the blue-ringed octopus. Watch nature videos about it. But don't buy one. They belong in the ocean, not in your home!

Glossary

biologist A scientist who studies living things.

gills The body part on a fish or other water animal that takes in water for oxygen.

organ A part of the body that has a special job or purpose, like the heart or lungs.

paralyze To make a person or animal unable to move or feel all or part of the body.

predator An animal that hunts another for food.

prey An animal that is hunted for food.

tide pool A rocky pool on the sea shore filled with seawater.

TTX Short for tetrodotoxin; a poison found in some animals that causes their prey to become paralyzed.

venom Poison produced by some animals, like blue-ringed octopuses.

Read More

Clarke, Ginjer L. *Watch out!: The World's Most Dangerous Creatures.* New York: Penguin Young Readers, 2012.

Lunis, Natalie. *Blue-ringed Octopus: Small But Deadly.* New York: Bearport, 2010.

Peterson, Judy Monroe. *Underwater Explorers: Marine Biologists.* New York: PowerKids Press, 2009.

Websites

Aquarium of the Pacific | Greater Blue-ringed Octopus
www.aquariumofpacific.org/onlinelearningcenter/species/greater_blue_ringed_octopus1

Laughing Kids Learn | Blue-Ringed Octopus
laughingkidslearn.com/tag/blue-ringed-octopus/

Nature | Animal Guide: Blue-Ringed Octopus
www.pbs.org/wnet/nature/interactives-extras/animal-guides/animal-guide-blue-ringed-octopus/2177/

Every effort has been made to ensure that these websites are appropriate for children. However, because of the nature of the Internet, it is impossible to guarantee that these sites will remain active indefinitely or that their contents will not be altered.

Index

About the Author

Elizabeth Raum has worked as a teacher, librarian, and writer. She enjoyed doing research and learning about poisonous animals, but she hopes never to find any of them near her house! Visit her website at: www.elizabethraum.net.